Shall we Dance?

There are six differences between these two pictures.
See if you can find them all.

Dot to Dot

Join the dots to see what the princess is holding.

Royal Mail

Princess Lily appears on her country's stamps!
All of these stamps are the same except one – can you find it?

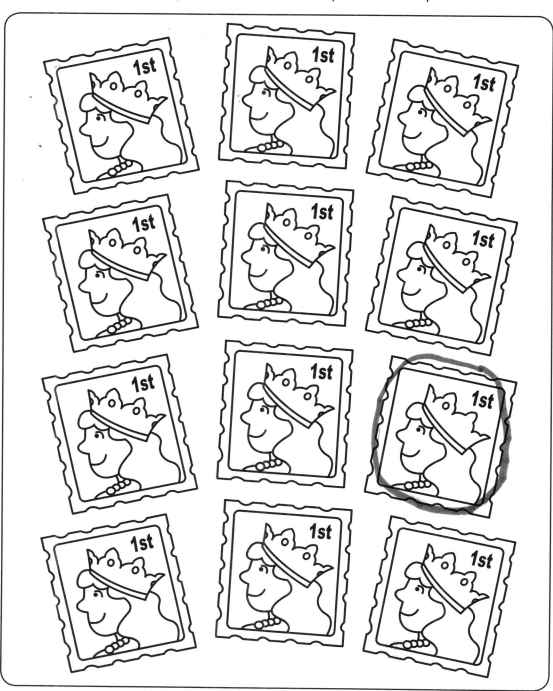

Belle of the Ball

Princess Phoebe is nearly ready for the ball.
Draw some pretty accessories in her hair to help her.

4

Love Story

How many smaller words can you spell, using the letters in the words below? Two are done already to help you.

HANDSOME

 PRINCE

PRICE

MAIDS

_____

_____

_____

_____

_____

_____

_____

_____

_____

_____

_____

_____

Brainy Janey

Can you help Princess Janey fill in the missing pictures so that every row, column and mini-grid has each of the four symbols?

Cute as a Kitten

Princess Emily just loves her pet kitten!
Colour the picture with your favourite colours.

Falling in Love

Can you turn LIKE into LOVE by changing one letter at a time?
Each change must use a real word. Use the clues to help you.

l i k e

_ _ _ _   A long walk

_ _ _ _   A home for bees

_ _ _ _   To exist or be alive

l o v e

Enchanted Princess

This princess has been turned into a swan by a wicked sorcerer.
Which of the silhouettes matches the picture exactly?

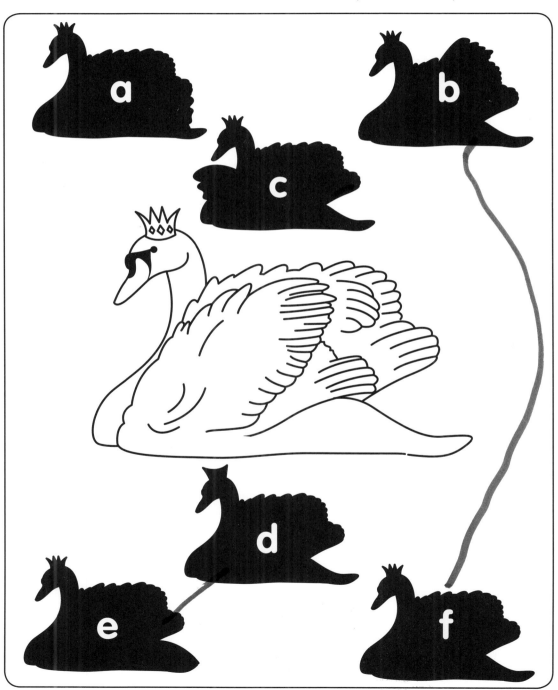

Be a Copycat

Can you copy the picture of the fairy princess onto the grid?
Use the lines to help you.

Laugh Out Loud

Cross out the words using the instructions below.
The words left will be the answer to the joke.

Where did the ice princess go to dance?

UNDER	TO	OUTSIDE
SUMMER	UP	PRINCE
PURSE	THE	CLUB
SNOW	WINTER	HOUSE!
PALACE!	POND!	BALL!

1. Words with more than 5 letters.

2. Words containing the letter U.

3. Words that begin with P.

Queenie

Here's a game you can play with your friends in your royal garden!

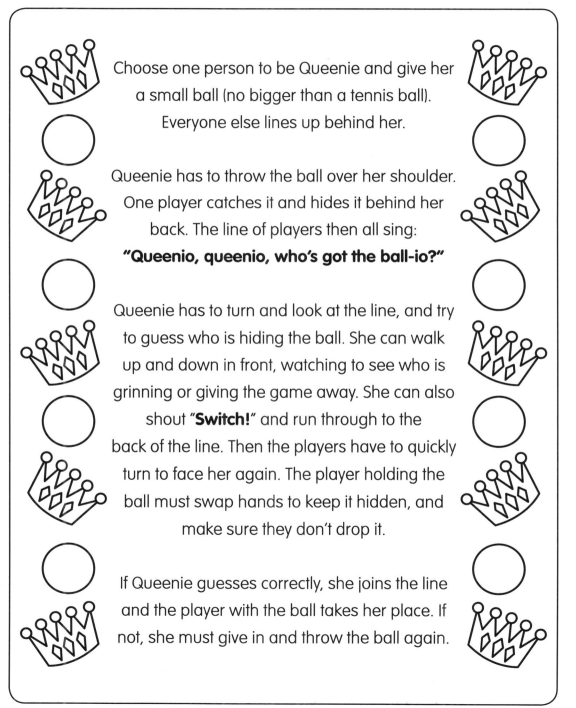

Choose one person to be Queenie and give her a small ball (no bigger than a tennis ball). Everyone else lines up behind her.

Queenie has to throw the ball over her shoulder. One player catches it and hides it behind her back. The line of players then all sing:
"Queenio, queenio, who's got the ball-io?"

Queenie has to turn and look at the line, and try to guess who is hiding the ball. She can walk up and down in front, watching to see who is grinning or giving the game away. She can also shout **"Switch!"** and run through to the back of the line. Then the players have to quickly turn to face her again. The player holding the ball must swap hands to keep it hidden, and make sure they don't drop it.

If Queenie guesses correctly, she joins the line and the player with the ball takes her place. If not, she must give in and throw the ball again.

Wicked!

Help the princess through the maze to get away from
the clutches of her wicked stepmother.

Petrova's Pets

Use the alphabet code to work out what each
of Princess Petrova's pets is called.

20 9 14 11 19

T I N K S

19 14 15 23 4 18 15 16

S N O W D R O P

2 21 20 20 15 14 19

B U T T O N S

18 1 6 6 12 5 19

R A F F L E S

1. **A**	5. **E**	9. **I**	13. **M**	17. **Q**	21. **U**	25. **Y**
2. **B**	6. **F**	10. **J**	14. **N**	18. **R**	22. **V**	26. **Z**
3. **C**	7. **G**	11. **K**	15. **O**	19. **S**	23. **W**	
4. **D**	8. **H**	12. **L**	16. **P**	20. **T**	24. **X**	

The Olden Days

A long time ago, princesses wore big dresses to show how rich they were.
Colour this one using the numbers to help you.

1 = red
2 = yellow
3 = purple

Choices, Choices

Which royal purse should Princess Vivienne choose?
Join the dots below and see which purse does not get crossed out.

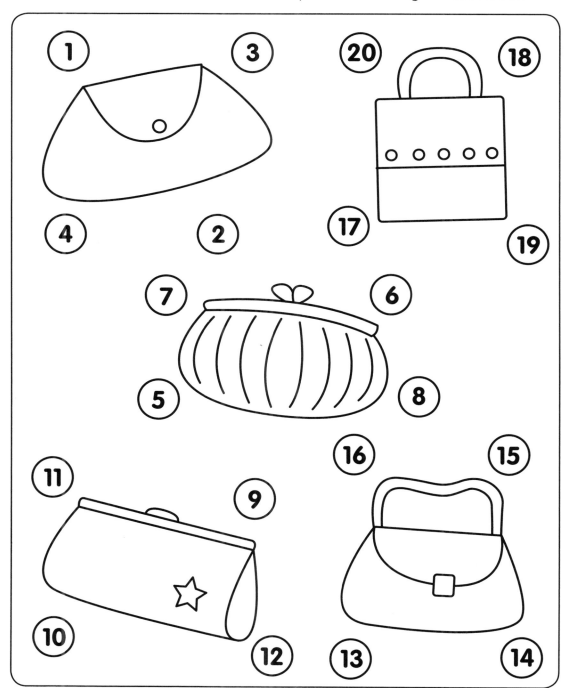

Double Trouble

Princesses Holly and Molly only like things that have a double letter in the name. Cross out the ones they don't like.

Hidden Treasure

Colour any section that has a * in it to find out
what is in the royal treasure box.

Time for a Kiss

This princess has found her handsome prince. All he needs is a kiss!
Find the silhouette that matches the picture exactly.

Far, Far Away

Which prince has travelled the farthest to meet Princess Adanna?
Add up the numbers on each pathway.

Dot to Dot

Join the dots to see what the princess is playing.

Mary, Mary

How many bells are hidden in Princess Mary's garden?

Use Your Head

Cross out the letters that appear twice to leave the name
of the princess this crown belongs to.

Window on the World

What can this princess see out of her window?
You decide and draw it in.

Two by Two

Help Princess Nimbulina up to her cloud castle by counting in 2s.

11   12

10

9

8

7

6

5

3   4

2

Be my Bridesmaid

Wouldn't it be fun to be a bridesmaid? Colour in
Princess Daisy's beautiful bridesmaid dress and flowers.

Fly Away

Which bird belongs to Princess Rosabel?

Firework Frenzy

This royal wedding has ended with a firework display.
Do the sums that are lit up in the sky.

6 + 7 =

9 − 4 =

12 + 5 =

16 − 3 =

3 + 8 =

15 − 5 =

Be a Copycat

Can you copy the picture of the royal elephant?
Use the grid lines to help you.

Poor Princess

Princess Tallulah is in a muddle. All of her shoes need matching into pairs. Can you help her?

Hidden Away

What is hiding in the royal forest?
Colour the sections with a * to find out.

Story Time

Arrange the pictures in the correct
order to tell the story properly.

Hide and Seek

Can you find the listed words hiding in the grid?
Watch out for two sneaky ones going diagonally.

```
e  h  g  o  w  n  b  r  g  s
n  s  n  e  z  b  l  u  o  p
c  a  r  r  i  a  g  e  t  e
h  a  p  w  y  l  m  f  q  l
a  v  k  g  x  l  o  i  a  l
n  f  d  i  e  t  z  v  w  f
t  q  u  o  n  y  b  x  e  k
e  c  v  m  r  g  p  d  l  i
d  i  p  u  m  p  k  i  n  s
h  c  u  r  s  e  c  n  s  s
```

ball   king
carriage   kiss
curse   love
enchanted   pumpkin
gown   spell

33

Dress the Princess

This party game is good for giggles! You need at least six players, and some dressing up clothes.

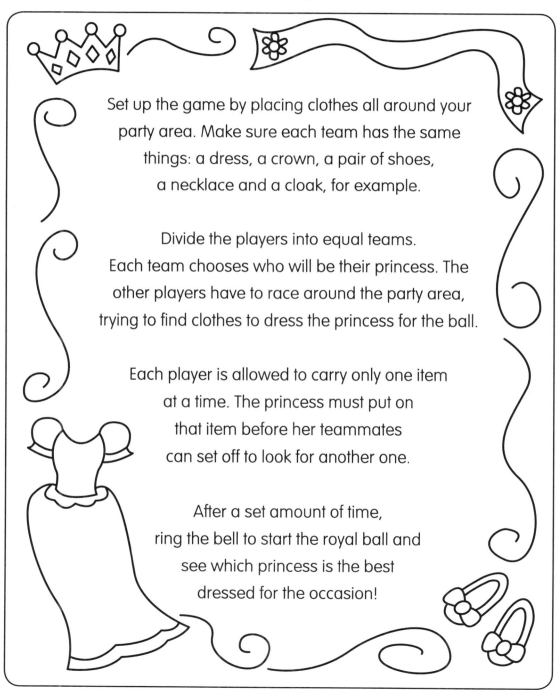

Set up the game by placing clothes all around your party area. Make sure each team has the same things: a dress, a crown, a pair of shoes, a necklace and a cloak, for example.

Divide the players into equal teams. Each team chooses who will be their princess. The other players have to race around the party area, trying to find clothes to dress the princess for the ball.

Each player is allowed to carry only one item at a time. The princess must put on that item before her teammates can set off to look for another one.

After a set amount of time, ring the bell to start the royal ball and see which princess is the best dressed for the occasion!

Mer-magic

Starting with the P, cross out every other letter in the seashell
to find out where the mermaid princess lives.

Coded Message

What message has Rapunzel passed to her beloved Prince?

My Hero

This princess has found her knight in shining armour!
Colour in the picture using the numbers to help you.

1 = pink

2 = silver

3 = blue

4 = yellow

Picture Puzzle

Use the picture clues to fill in the words.
The letters in the shaded squares will spell another word for 'gown'.

Royal Wedding

There are five differences between these two pictures.
See if you can find them all.

Dot to Dot

Join the dots to see what the princess has in her hand.

Fairy Story

Colour in the boxes that contain o, s and b to leave letters spelling the best part of many princess stories.

41

Mermaid Princess

Who is this princess playing with under the sea?
Draw lots of creatures to help her have fun.

Flower Garden

Count how many of each type of flower Princess Daisy
has in her garden. Write the totals in the boxes.

Girl's Best Friend

Can you see which of these diamond earrings matches the one in the circle?

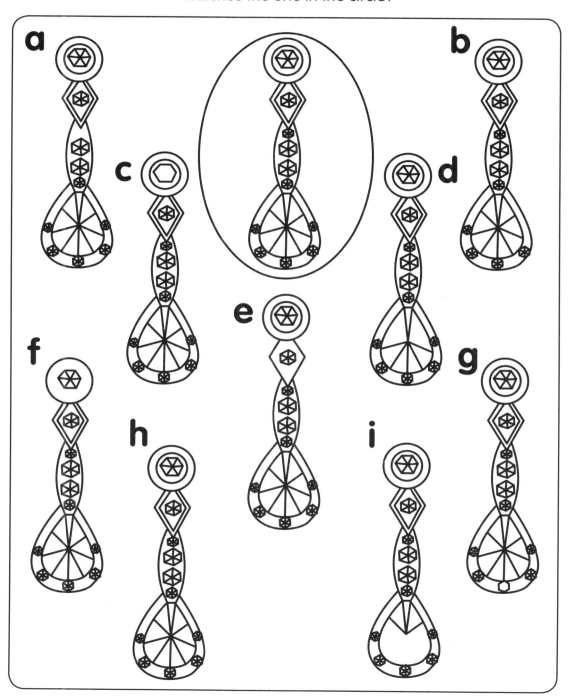

One for You

Imagine you are princess for the day. What would your dress be like?
Colour the accessories to match, too.

Ring Ring

Which ring will Princess Alicia wear to the party?
Use the clues to work it out.

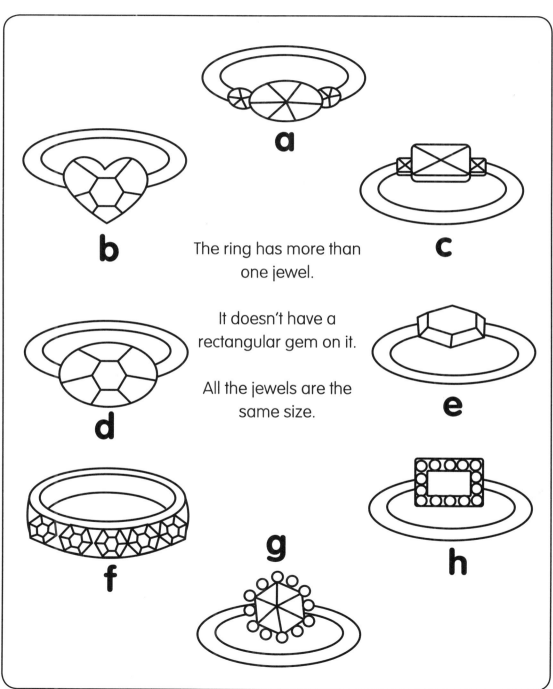

a

b

c

The ring has more than
one jewel.

It doesn't have a
rectangular gem on it.

All the jewels are the
same size.

d

e

f

g

h

From the Heart

Princess Amy just loves everything heart-shaped.
Can you help her find a way through this maze?

Be a Copycat

Can you copy the picture of the royal swan onto the grid?
Use the lines to help you.

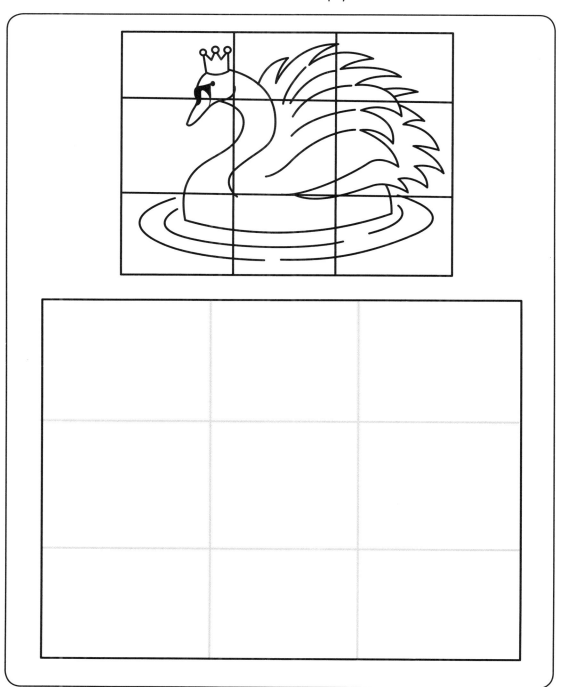

Maths Lesson

Even a princess needs to learn maths.
Help Princess Tanisha fill in the number squares on the whiteboard.

Brilliant Birthdays

Match each of the princesses to the birthday cake she likes best.

Royal Whispers

Can you talk just like a true princess?
Have fun trying with this game.

The game is best with at least five players.
You should all sit in a circle. The first player
whispers something to the player next to her.
Make sure none of the others can hear.

Try to think of something very royal, and say
it in your poshest princess voice. Start with
something like, "Princess Petrona would be
most obliged if you would attend her
pony party at the royal stables."

The second player has to whisper the message
to her neighbour, who whispers it to the next
person, right around the circle until the
last person gets the message.

No one is allowed to repeat the whisper, so if
you don't hear properly, you must just say what
you think you heard. The last player says the
message out loud; it may have changed
quite a lot from when it started!

What's My Name?

Find out the name of this princess by filling in the coded letters.
For example, E6 = p.

	1	**2**	**3**	**4**	**5**	**6**
A	q	n	o	e	d	m
B	a	l	b	g	s	i
C	u	s	d	c	v	b
D	b	t	r	y	n	h
E	c	i	o	e	l	p
F	k	f	w	a	t	u

__ __ __ __ __ __
B5   C1   A2   E2   D2   F4

Baby Belle

Colour any section that has a * in it to
find out what the picture shows.

Nature Trail

Princess Magnolia is picking flowers in the garden. Draw a path to collect them all, but do not cross over any line you have already drawn.

Rhyme Time

Draw lines to connect the objects outside the picture
to things inside the picture that rhyme with them.

Arabian Nights

The Tales of the Arabian Nights are full of princes and princesses.
Colour in the picture using the numbers to help you.

1 = blue
2 = yellow
3 = green

Royal Riddle

Solve the riddle to find the name of Princess Peony's pet pony.

My first is in 'red', and in 'riding', and 'hood'.

My second's in 'goat' but isn't in 'good'.

My third is a letter found in 'ice', 'gift' and 'guitar'.

My fourth's in the 'alphabet' just after 'r'.

My last letter's in 'shy' but isn't in 'his'.

My name is a flower, do you know what it is?

Beautiful Butterflies

Match up the butterflies so that each one finds its identical twin.

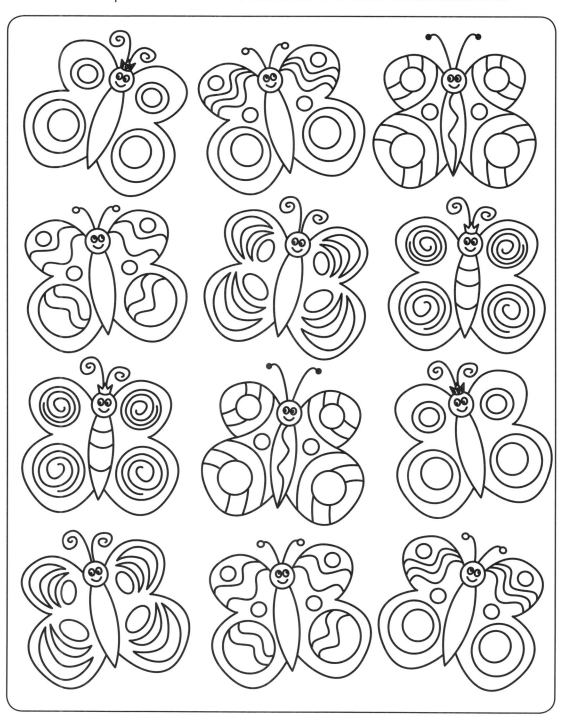

Kiss that Frog!

Do you think you could kiss an enchanted frog to turn him into a prince?
Do it the easy way with this game.

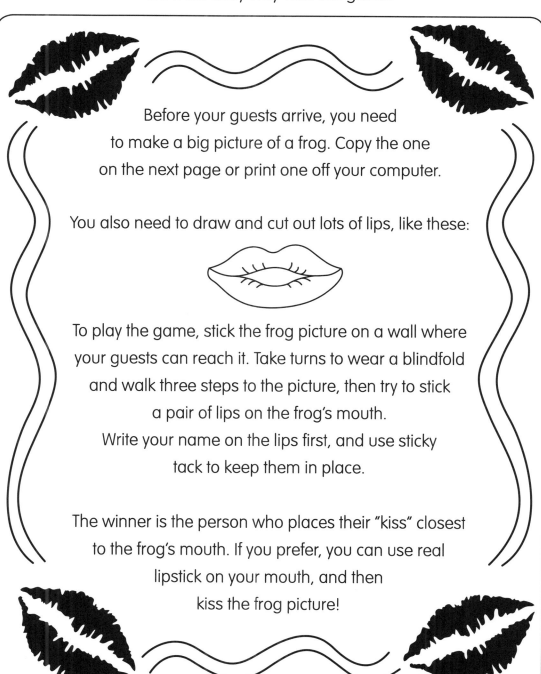

Before your guests arrive, you need
to make a big picture of a frog. Copy the one
on the next page or print one off your computer.

You also need to draw and cut out lots of lips, like these:

To play the game, stick the frog picture on a wall where
your guests can reach it. Take turns to wear a blindfold
and walk three steps to the picture, then try to stick
a pair of lips on the frog's mouth.
Write your name on the lips first, and use sticky
tack to keep them in place.

The winner is the person who places their "kiss" closest
to the frog's mouth. If you prefer, you can use real
lipstick on your mouth, and then
kiss the frog picture!

Froggy Fun

Can you copy the picture of the frog prince onto the grid?
Use the lines to help you.

Design-a-Dress

Add your own decorations to this princess's pretty party dress.

Home Sweet Home

Follow the correct path to the doorway and you will spell somewhere a princess might live.

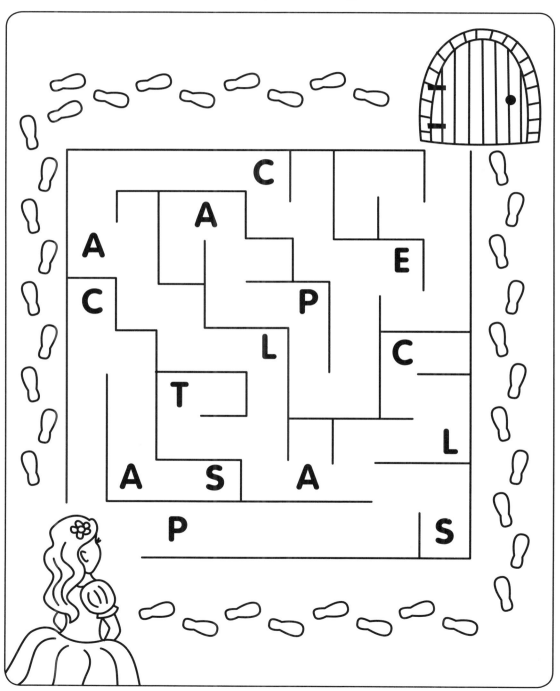

Nearly Midnight

Help Princess Thea run away from the ball
and find the correct path back to her own bed.

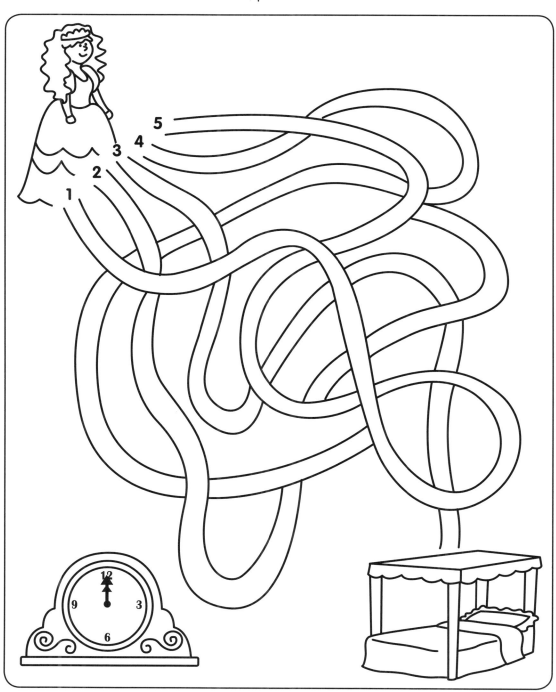

My Royal Pony

Princess Lastri loves her pony to pieces!
Colour the picture to make it even more pretty.

Rescue Mission

Which of the keys should the Prince use to try to rescue the princess?

Royal Rings

Here's a great game for your next princess party.
You need string or wool, and dressing up "diamond" rings.

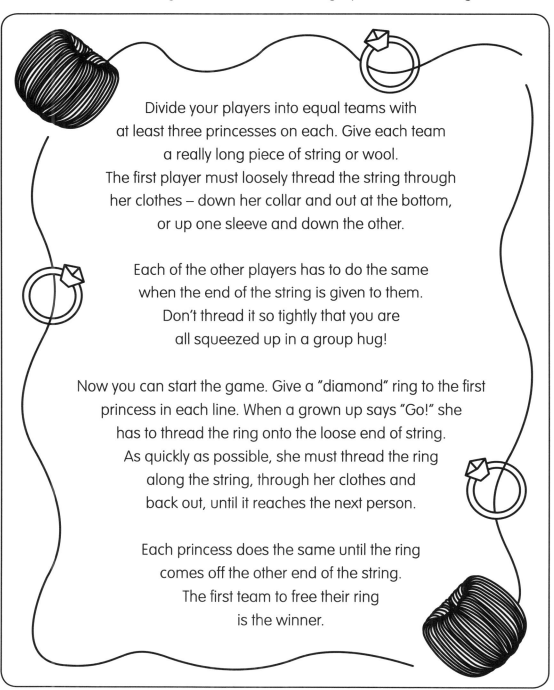

Divide your players into equal teams with
at least three princesses on each. Give each team
a really long piece of string or wool.
The first player must loosely thread the string through
her clothes – down her collar and out at the bottom,
or up one sleeve and down the other.

Each of the other players has to do the same
when the end of the string is given to them.
Don't thread it so tightly that you are
all squeezed up in a group hug!

Now you can start the game. Give a "diamond" ring to the first
princess in each line. When a grown up says "Go!" she
has to thread the ring onto the loose end of string.
As quickly as possible, she must thread the ring
along the string, through her clothes and
back out, until it reaches the next person.

Each princess does the same until the ring
comes off the other end of the string.
The first team to free their ring
is the winner.

Sleeping Beauty

Study the picture of Princess Maddie and see which
of the jigsaw pieces fits in the gap.

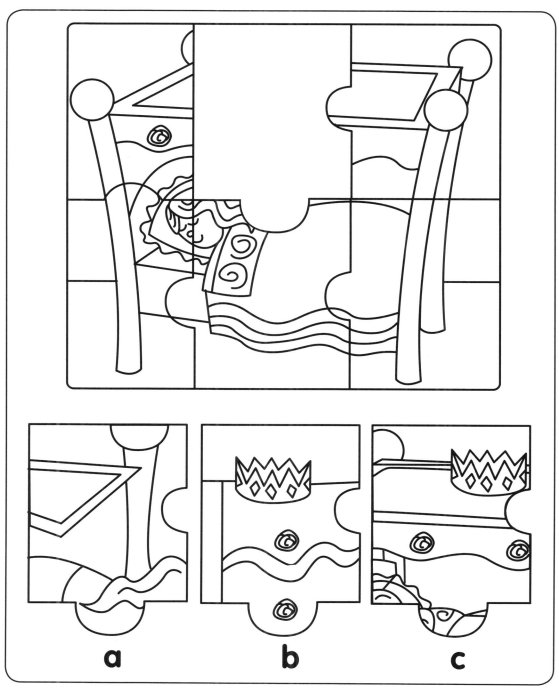

a

b

c

Princess Diary

Cross out the letters that appear twice to leave
the name of the princess who writes in this diary.

Melissa's Maths

Princess Melissa loves maths when it's number codes like this.
Work out the answers with her.

1 = ♡
2 = ❀
3 = ◈
4 = 👄
5 = 🍦
6 = 🦋
7 = ☄
8 = 🌀
9 = ✹

🍦 + ◈ = ☐

✹ - ❀ = ☐

♡ X 🦋 = ☐

👄 + ☄ = ☐

🌀 - 🦋 = ☐

Finders, Keepers

Princess Lucy has found something pretty. Colour the circles to find it.

1 = orange 2 = yellow 3 = green

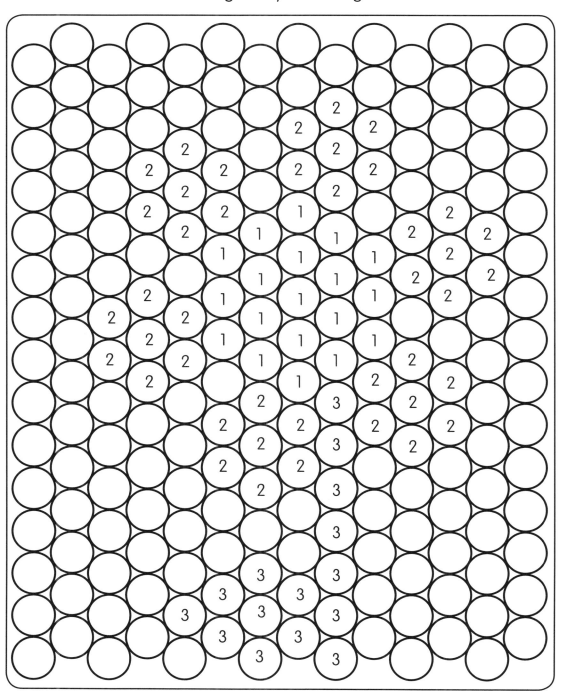

Flower Princess

Colour in the flowers to keep
this flower princess happy.

Round and Round

Starting with the circled 'T', go twice around the circle (clockwise) writing every other letter to find a hidden message.

Crowning Glory

Which of Princess Amalia's crowns matches the shadow on the wall?

Be a Copycat

Can you copy the picture of the palace onto the grid?
Use the lines to help you.

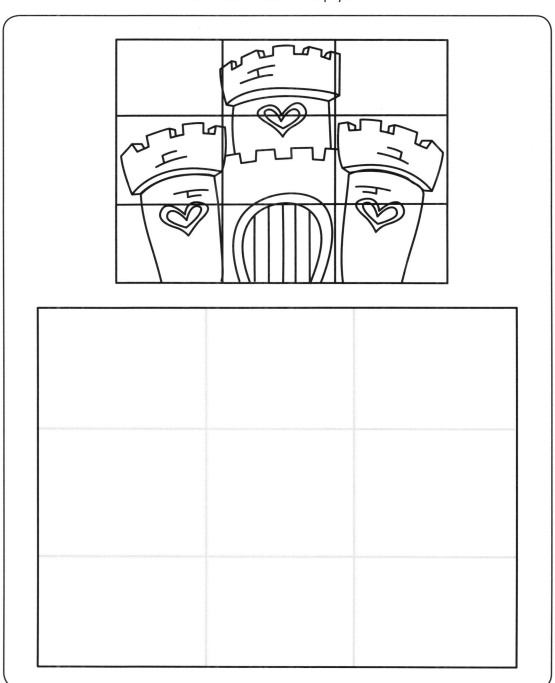

Tiara Tangle

How many tiaras are tangled up in this pile?

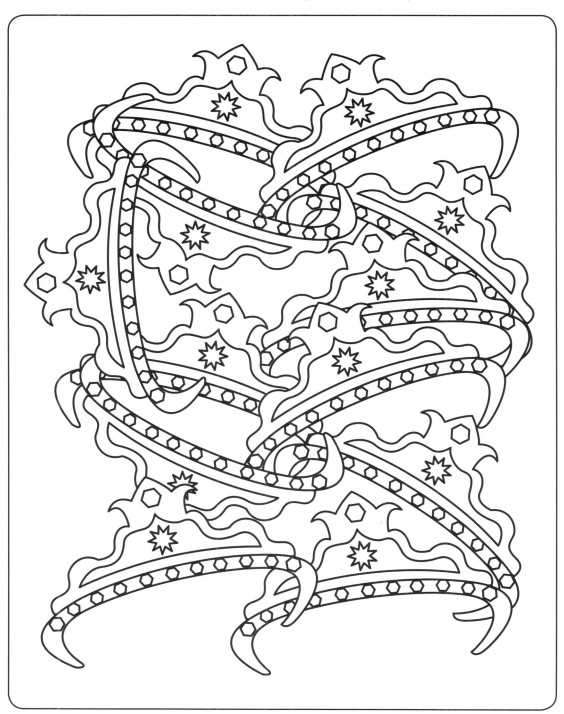

Answers

1.

3.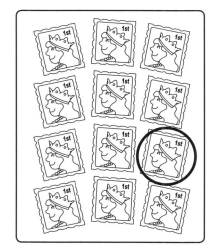

5. Here are some you might have thought of: cap, ship, head, sand, mice, moan, dance, scone, shrimp, spend.

6.

8. like-hike-hive-live-love

9. f

11. To the snow ball!

13.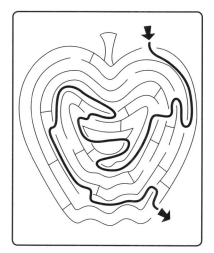

14. Tinks; Snowdrop; Buttons; Raffles

16. Princess Vivienne should choose the purse in the bottom right.

17. They don't like the ladybird, mouse, pear or wand. They do like the apple, teddy, rabbit and bee.

19. e

20. 5 + 5 + 1 + 6 = 17
    1 + 4 + 6 + 3 = 14
    10 + 2 + 1 + 5 = 18

22. There are 8 hidden bells.

23. The crown belongs to Princess Bonita.

25.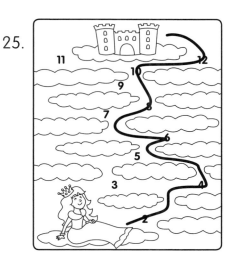

27. B

28. 6 + 7 = 13
    9 − 4 = 5
    12 + 5 = 17
    16 − 3 = 13
    3 + 8 = 11
    15 − 5 = 10

32. C, D, A, B

33.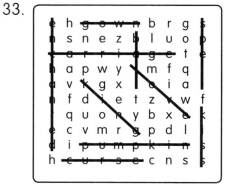

35. Shipwreck

36. Rescue me at midnight.

38. 1. dream
    2. crown
    3. queen
    4. purse
    5. rings

The shaded squares
spell 'dress'.

43.

44. h

46. f

39.

47.

41. They all lived happily
    ever after.

49.

50. 1b, 2c, 3a

52. Sunita

54.

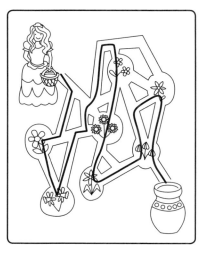

55. car-star
ring-king
bone-throne
log-dog
bean-queen
clown-crown

57. Daisy

62.

63. 3

65. c

67. c

68. Megan

73. e

75. 12

69.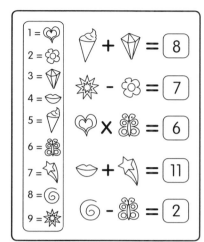

70.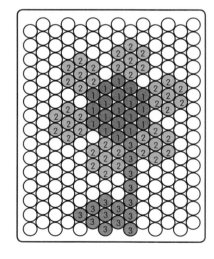

72. There are unicorns
    in the royal grounds.